Bubba
texas cuisine

© The Great Texas Line Press, PO Box 11105, Fort Worth, TX 76110
1-800-73TEXAS • WWW.GREATTEXASLINE.COM

"Of the world's four great cuisines – French, Italian, Chinese and Texan – only the later has a recipe beginning, `First, dig a three-foot-deep hole...'"

So wrote Jerry Flemmons, a Fort Worth playwright, biographer, editor and bon vivant who brightened many lives before moving to a better place. No one would ever accuse Jerry being unbiased when it came to food or Texas, but he might just have had something. Of course, he probably would have been the first to admit that Texas cuisine has not traveled well. We hope this modest volume is a step in the right direction.

While none of this book's recipes lists a shovel or pickax among required utensils, I have endeavored to capture the essence of Texas cooking with an assortment of popular and traditional dishes, as well as a few nouveau ones worth sharing.

For our Cordon Bubba collection we tapped people like Sondra Cochran, an early booster of this project; Carmelita Bevill, who doubled as copy editor; Vicky Blackman Walker, who without too much pressure divulged her long-secret BBQ sauce recipe; Betty Hill, who shared with us a trove known as the Stringer family recipes; Juanita Gonzales, who set us straight on autentico Tex-Mex; my wife, Amrita, a.k.a. Rita Mae, who provided illustrations; and Meda Kessler, who spun her design magic.

Some of the original dishes were created, and graciously provided, by Chef Grady Spears. In the words of Texas Monthly, Spears has "melded mythic and modern Texas" to craft a distinctive cowboy cuisine. Author of "Cowboy in the Kitchen," Spears is now the chef-owner of Fort Worth's Chisholm Club and the revamped Nutt House Restaurant on Granbury's historic courthouse square.

We asked Lubbock native Keith Faulkner, who is chef at New Orleans' Plimsoll Club, to apply his special touch to such popular Texas dishes as fried catfish, jalapeno hush puppies and bread pudding. It's clear from them that Faulkner has not forsaken his Texas heritage.

This slender volume is by no means the last word in Texas cuisine. Should it, however, provide sufficient spark to ignite an interest in Lone Star eats in, say, a recovering Yankee, I would consider our mission accomplished.

Barry Shlachter
Fort Worth, Texas

Cordon Bubba

texas cuisine

Table of Contents

Easy
GRAZING

 APPETIZERS

Guacamole

Contributed by Juanita Rodriguez of Fort
Worth and Moreles

Combine all the ingredients by
hand. Do not use food processor or
sieve.

Put the avocado seed in the top of
the dip, to keep mixture from
turning brown.

Cover, chill and serve (with or
without the seed), as condiment for
fajitas, dip for tortilla chips or
refreshing summer side dish.

- ⊠ 2 ripe avocados,
  peeled and mashed
- ⊠ 1 bunch green
  onions, chopped
  finely (including a lot
  of the stalks)
- ⊠ 1 medium tomato,
  diced
- ⊠ Salt to taste
- ⊠ Cayenne pepper to
  taste
- ⊠ Juice of 1/2 lime
- ⊠ Cilantro to garnish

Seven-layer bean dip

- 3 ripened avocadoes
- 2 tsps. lemon or lime juice
- Salt, black pepper to taste
- 1 cup sour cream
- 1 cup mayonnaise
- 2 tbsps. taco seasoning
- 1/2 tsp. garlic powder
- Hot pepper sauce, to taste
- 1 can of refried beans
- 3 tbsps. chopped onions
- 4 tomatoes, chopped
- 7 oz. black olives, chopped
- 8 oz. Cheddar cheese, grated
- Tortilla chips

An adaptation of several favorite versions of this dip, which is popular at Texas holiday gatherings, family get-togethers and tailgate parties. Serve with tortilla chips and long-necks.

Mash pulp of peeled avocadoes in bowl, add juice, salt, pepper, one chopped tomato, chopped onion and hot sauce, then set aside.

Separately, mix sour cream, mayonnaise and spices, then set aside.

In a 9-inch pie pan, equivalent glass casserole dish or platter, spread bean's as first layer. Second layer is avocado mixture. Cover with sour cream/mayonnaise mixture. Sprinkle chopped tomatoes, green onions and cheese. Top with black olives. Serves 10.

CORDON BUBBA TIP

To enliven, use jalapeño refried beans.

Texas caviar

It's good luck, bordering on a necessity, to eat black-eyed peas on New Year's. And this legume, also known as a cow pea, happens to taste good. Particularly when transformed into Texas Caviar.

Chop vegetables; add black-eyed peas and picante sauce.

Can be served immediately as a side dish or dip for tortilla chips, or place in covered container and refrigerated overnight.

CORDON BUBBA TIP ⭐

Enliven mixture with 2 seeded and minced jalapeños, 1/4 cup chopped pitted black olives, small jar of chopped pimiento, and substitute wine vinegar for the regular variety.

⭐ 1/3 cup diced onion

⭐ 1/3 tsp. salt

⭐ 2 cans black-eyed peas, a.k.a. cowpeas

⭐ 3 tomatoes, diced

⭐ 1 cloves garlic, minced

⭐ 1 green pepper, diced

⭐ 1/4 cup fresh cilantro

⭐ 1 16-oz. jar picante sauce

⭐ 1/4 cup vinegar

Stuffed jalapeños

- ⊠ 8 oz. cream cheese, softened
- ⊠ 10 oz. jar whole jalapeños
- ⊠ 1 small onion, chopped

Contributed by Linda Montgomery of Fort Worth

Drain jalapeños and halve lengthwise. Remove stems, seeds and pulp. Cover with water and soak at least one hour. (Overnight for milder version.)

Mix cream cheese with onion.

Stuff jalapenos with mixture.

Serve chilled. Feed 4-5 Texans, 8-10 Yankees.

CORDON BUBBA TIP ⊠

To avoid jalapeño-burning-finger syndrome, consider investing in a pair of those latex kitchen gloves for use when handling the peppers.

Salsa

Heat oil in saucepan, then sauté onion until transparent.

Pour into bowl, combine all ingredients but cilantro, cover and refrigerate at least one hour.

Just before serving — at room temperature — add cilantro leaves.

- ⚝ 1 tbsp. vegetable oil
- ⚝ 1 small onion, finely diced
- ⚝ 2 large tomatoes, diced
- ⚝ 1 small green chili, seeded and chopped
- ⚝ 1 jalapeño, or to taste, stemmed, seeded and chopped
- ⚝ 3 tbsps. cilantro leaves
- ⚝ Salt, pepper to taste
- ⚝ 3 tbsps. lemon juice

Salsa verde

- ☒ 1 lb. tomatillos, husks removed
- ☒ 1 cup loosely packed cilantro leaves, roughly chopped
- ☒ 5 jalapeño peppers, diced
- ☒ 6 scallions, chopped
- ☒ 2 cloves garlic, minced
- ☒ 2 tbsps. fresh lime juice
- ☒ 1/2 tsp. salt
- ☒ 1/8 tsp. freshly ground black pepper

Contributed by Grady H. Spears, chef, Reata Restaurant, Alpine and Fort Worth

Add tomatillos to boiling water; cook 3 to 5 minutes, until just soft.

Drain. Let cool, chop into 1/2-inch pieces and place in a bowl.

Toss with remaining ingredients.

Refrigerate for several hours before serving.

Salsa will keep refrigerated 2 to 3 days.

Armadillo eggs

Remove pepper stems, slice peppers lengthwise, rinse out seeds.

Stuff with cheese.

Flatten sausages and shape into patties and wrap them around stuffed peppers.

Bake at 450 degrees until sausage is browned.

Drain on paper towels. Wrap biscuit dough around each piece, bake at 450 degrees until lightly browned.

- 10 whole jalapeño peppers
- 12 oz. grated Cheddar or Monterrey jack cheese
- 1 lb. hot ground sausage
- 10 canned biscuits

Chile con queso

- 🌟 1 large onion, chopped
- 🌟 1 bell pepper, red or green, chopped
- 🌟 2 tbsps. margarine
- 🌟 2 tbsps. flour
- 🌟 1-1/2 cups evaporated milk
- 🌟 1 clove garlic, minced
- 🌟 1 tsp. chili powder
- 🌟 1 10-oz. can tomatoes and chilies
- 🌟 2 lbs. of grated or cubed processed American cheese

Melt margarine in saucepan and fry garlic, onion and bell pepper.

Add flour, chili powder, optional jalapeño and cook till thick.

Gradually add canned milk.

Melt cheese in double boiler and add to first mixture.

Stir until well blended. Should not be allowed to boil.

Serves 12. Great as a tortilla chip dip or sauce for broccoli, etc.

CORDON BUBBA TIP 🌟

Variations: Instead of canned tomatoes and chilies, use 1 diced tomato and 2 jalapeños, remove stems and seeds, then chop. Try a 50-50 mixture of Cheddar and Monterey jack substituting for processed cheese.

Tortilla pinwheels

Contributed by Jan Fennell of Arlington

Blend cream cheese, onion, sour cream, (optional chili powder), hot sauce and chopped green chiles.

Spread thickly over tortillas. Roll up.

Chill for six hours or overnight.

Before serving, slice crosswise, making pinwheel pieces. Yields 3 dozen.

CORDON BUBBA TIP ⭐

Place a bowl of salsa nearby for dipping.

- ⭐ 2 packages cream cheese
- ⭐ 1 tsp. grated onion
- ⭐ 2 tbsps. sour cream (or non-fat variety)
- ⭐ Hot sauce to taste
- ⭐ 3 jalapeños, remove stems and seeds, dice
- ⭐ 12 flour tortillas
- ⭐ 1 tsp. chili powder, optional

Jalapeño jelly

- ☒ 1 cup ripe red bell peppers, seeded and finely chopped

- ☒ 6 jalapeño peppers, seeded and finely chopped

- ☒ 1-1/2 cups cider vinegar

- ☒ 6 cups sugar

- ☒ 6 oz. of liquid pectin, or equivalent dry pectin

- ☒ (Optional: green food coloring)

CORDON BUBBA TIP ☒

Use as a condiment, relish or smeared over cream cheese on crackers as guests-at-the-door, quick-assembly hors d'oeuvres.

Put jars in boiling water for a minute or place them in dishwasher and remove when still hot.

Using latex gloves when handling jalapeños, chop both types of peppers and throw in a pot.

Add vinegar and sugar and boil for 25 minutes. Don't let it boil over. Skim if necessary.

Cool 15 minutes, stir in pectin and boil for another 2 minutes.

Test jelling by placing small amount on a saucer and put in freezer for a few minutes.

If still liquid, continue boiling, then test until jelled. Before ladling into hot jars, stir so that shredded peppers are suspended. Yields five 6-oz. self-sealing mason jars.

Calf fries

At a banquet before the start of every Southwestern Livestock Show and Rodeo, Fort Worth's century-plus institution, calf fries are always the first appetizer served.

Scald calf fries for 3 to 4 minutes. Peel off membrane. If desired, cut into bite-sized pieces or medallions, then dry.

Mix salt, pepper and flour.

Dip in beaten egg, dredge in seasoned flour and fry, preferably deep fried, until brown in hot oil (or grease or shortening).

- 1 doz. calf testicles
- 1 egg, slightly beaten
- Flour
- Salt, pepper
- Bacon grease, vegetable oil or shortening

Cream of avocado soup

- 3 ripened avocados
- 2 tsps. lime juice
- Salt, black pepper to taste
- 1/4 tsp. powdered ginger
- 2 cups chicken broth
- 4 tsps. dry sherry (optional)
- 1-1/3 cups heavy cream

Puree all ingredients in blender except cream.

Stir in cream.

Chill.

Cream of jalapeño and cilantro soup

Contributed by Grady H. Spears, chef, Reata Restaurant, Alpine and Fort Worth

We sampled this soup on a trip to Big Bend country and knew it must be part of this cookbook. If you know of a richer Texas soup, let us know.

Sauté jalapeños, onion and garlic in a large sauce pan well oiled with clarified butter.

Add avocado, tomato and cream, but quickly lower heat before cream breaks.

Reduce by one-third on low heat, about 25 minutes.

Add salt and pepper to taste.

Add cilantro just before serving.

Serves 6 Yankees or 4 Texans.

- ☒ Clarified butter
- ☒ 5 diced jalapeños
- ☒ 1 diced avocado
- ☒ 16 oz.. tomatoes, chopped, in juice
- ☒ *1/2 gallon cream* (this is not a misprint)
- ☒ 2 gloves of garlic, minced
- ☒ Salt and white pepper
- ☒ 1 bunch of cilantro, diced

Tortilla soup

- 🗙 5 corn tortillas, cut into strips
- 🗙 Vegetable oil
- 🗙 1 medium onion, chopped
- 🗙 1 4-oz. can chopped green chilies
- 🗙 3 gloves garlic, crushed
- 🗙 3 tomatoes, pureed
- 🗙 1 can beef broth
- 🗙 2 cans chicken broth
- 🗙 1-1/2 cups tomato juice
- 🗙 1 tsp. ground cumin
- 🗙 1 tsp. chili powder
- 🗙 Salt, pepper to taste
- 🗙 Cayenne pepper, to taste
- 🗙 2 tbsps. cilantro (coriander)
- 🗙 1/2 cup Cheddar or Jack cheese, grated

Fry tortilla strips in oil until crispy and brown (or bake at 400 degrees until brown).

In soup pot, sauté onion, chilies and garlic in 2 tablespoons of oil, add pureed tomatoes, broth, tomato juice, spices, cilantro and bring to boil.

Lower heat, simmer 1 hour.

Add tortillas and cheese, simmer 10-15 minutes.

Garnish with additional fresh cilantro.

Welfare soup

Contributed by Roland Lindsey, San Saba and Arlington.

A stick-to-your-ribs soup that can warm up a winter day or see you through a lot of month left at the end of your money.

In large stock pot, sauté diced onion in oil, add ground meat and cook till browned.

Add lentils, tomatoes and mixed vegetables. Add enough water to cover.

Season to taste with salt, pepper, a splash of ketchup, then check fridge for whatever else might be available.

Bring mixture to a boil, cover and let simmer for 45 minutes, stirring occasionally.

CORDON BUBBA TIP ⭐

Leftover corn, peas, potatoes, carrots can be used, along with a healthy squirt of steak sauce or any other handy seasoning.

⭐ 1 lb. dried lentils, rinsed in water

⭐ 1 lb. ground turkey (or hamburger or leftover chicken breast)

⭐ 1 onion, diced

⭐ 1 tbsp. cooking oil

⭐ 1 28-oz. can peeled tomatoes

⭐ 2 15-oz. cans mixed vegetables

⭐ 3 oz. of salsa, mild, medium or hot to taste

Siders

⭐ SIDE DISHES
BISCUITS

cilantro

Buttermilk biscuits

Contributed by Sondra Cochran, Fort Worth and Stamford

Nobody is going to make biscuits as good as a Texan's own mother. But for those of you not blessed with a Lone Star meemaw in the kitchen, we called on a genuine one to supply this recipe.

- ☒ 2 cups flour
- ☒ 4 tsps. baking powder
- ☒ 3 tbsps. vegetable shortening
- ☒ 1/2 tsp. salt
- ☒ 1 cup buttermilk

Combine flour, baking powder and salt.

Mix in shortening with fingers or pastry blender.

Make a well and add buttermilk.

Mix all ingredients well.

Roll to 1-inch thickness on floured board and cut to desired size.

Bake at 500 degrees 8-10 minutes or until lightly browned. Makes 6 medium biscuits.

Sweet potato pone

- ★ 2 cups grated sweet potato
- ★ 1 cup milk
- ★ 1 cup sugar
- ★ 2 eggs
- ★ 2 tbsps. butter

Based on the John B. Wilkin family recipe, Washington County

Combine all ingredients.

Bake in ovenproof casserole dish for 45 minutes or until set.

★ **CORDON BUBBA TIP**

Add 1 cup chopped pecans.

Jalapeño cornbread

Texans took a perfectly good Southern food and made it better.

Mix everything well and pour into greased 9-by-13-inch baking pan.

Bake at 425 degrees for about 25 minutes or until done. Serves 6-9.

⭐ **CORDON BUBBA TIP**

Upgrade with 2/3 cup of fresh or frozen corn kernels, or small handful of bacon bits or diced pimiento.

- ⭐ 3 cups yellow cornmeal
- ⭐ 4 tbsps. flour
- ⭐ 2 tsps. baking powder
- ⭐ 1 tsp. salt
- ⭐ 1 cup milk or buttermilk
- ⭐ 2 eggs, beaten
- ⭐ 2 tbsps. sugar
- ⭐ 1/2 cup chopped onion
- ⭐ 1/4 cup chopped jalapeños, fresh or pickled
- ⭐ 3/4 cup grated Cheddar cheese
- ⭐ 1/2 cup vegetable oil

Cheese grits

- 6 cups water
- 1 lb. American processed cheese, grated
- 1-1/2 cups quick (not instant) grits
- 1-1/2 sticks butter (or margarine)
- 3 eggs, well beaten
- 1 tsp. salt
- 1 tsp. seasoning salt
- 8-10 shakes of Tabasco sauce
- Paprika

Contributed by Carmelita Bevill, Conroe and Fort Worth.

Bring water to a boil, add grits and turn down heat.

Cook 5 minutes or until thick.

Add butter (or margarine), mix well, then add eggs and mix well.

Add grated cheese and mix until cheese has melted.

Add salt, mix, then do the same with seasoning salt and Tabasco.

Pour in 9-by-13-inch baking dish, sprinkle with paprika, cook at 250 degrees for 1 hour.

Serves 12 Yankees, 8 Texans.

Cherry coke salad

Contributed by Marjorie Strickland, San Antonio

Place drained fruit in a bowl.

Heat fruit juice to boiling point.

Stir in gelatin and keep stirring until dissolved.

Add cola, chill until slightly thickened.

Stir in fruit and nuts, then pour into gelatin mold.

Chill until firm.

Serves 12.

- 1 (16-oz.) can pitted Bing cherries
- 1 (20-oz.) can crushed pineapple
- 2 cups fruit juice and water (juice from cherry and pineapple cans)
- 2 regular packages black cherry gelatin
- 1 (12-oz.) can cola
- 1 cup chopped pecans

West Texas beans

- 🎫 1 lb. dried pinto beans, soaked overnight
- 🎫 1 onion, diced
- 🎫 Salt pork
- 🎫 2 tbsps. bacon drippings
- 🎫 Fresh ground pepper, to taste
- 🎫 4 canned (sliced) jalapeños or 2 fresh (sliced) ones.
- 🎫 2 or 3 cloves of garlic, minced
- 🎫 2 tbsps. fresh cilantro, chopped
- 🎫 Any longneck beer brewed in Texas

Contributed by Vickie Blackman Walker, Anson and Fort Worth

What would a chuckwagon dinner or a true Texas barbecue be without a plate of beans?

Cover beans with water and beer; add rest of ingredients and simmer slowly for at least three hours or until beans are tender.

Hush puppies

Contributed by Keith Faulkner, Lubbock and New Orleans

Combine all ingredients in a bowl.

Mix and then let them rest for 30 minutes.

With a 1-inch ice cream scoop, drop hush puppies into hot oil (370 degrees).

Cook until golden brown.

Drain on paper towels.

- ☒ 2 cups cornmeal
- ☒ 1 cup flour
- ☒ 2 eggs
- ☒ 1 cup buttermilk
- ☒ 1 tbsp. melted butter
- ☒ 1/4 cup sugar
- ☒ 1/4 cup chopped, seeded jalapeños
- ☒ 1/4 tsp. baking soda
- ☒ 2 tsps. pepper
- ☒ 1/4 cup chopped green onions
- ☒ 1/2 cup chopped onion
- ☒ 1 cup corn

German potato salad

- ★ 3 lbs. red-skinned potatoes, scrub but don't peel
- ★ 1/4 cup cider vinegar
- ★ 6 slices lean bacon, cooked and crumbled
- ★ 1 tsp. sugar
- ★ 1 onion, diced
- ★ 1 tsp. chopped pimiento
- ★ Ground black pepper, salt to taste
- ★ 3 tbsps. chopped parsley or cilantro
- ★ Dill seed
- ★ 2 eggs, hard-boiled

Cook and drain potatoes; slice into 1/2-inch scallops.

Cool slightly, add vinegar.

Slice onions and separate into rings.

Combine all ingredients, garnishing with parsley, dill seed and sliced hard-boiled eggs.

Serves 6-8

Fried okra

Contributed by Gertrude Albertina "Gertie" Poirot, Wichita Falls

Wash okra, remove stems; cut into 1/2-inch slices.

Toss okra pieces into beaten egg, then drop into bowl with cornmeal, flour, salt and pepper.

Make sure pieces are thoroughly coated.

Pan fry in 1/4-inch of hot oil over moderate heat until browned; drain on paper towels.

Serves 4-6

- ⭐ 1 lb. fresh okra
- ⭐ 1 egg, beaten
- ⭐ 3/4 cup cornmeal
- ⭐ 1/4 cup flour
- ⭐ Salt, pepper to taste
- ⭐ 2 cups cooking oil (or bacon grease)

Serious

VITTLES

Chili: Official
State Dish
• No beans
• As hot as you
   like.

Chicken-fried steak

No one loves chicken-fried steaks more than Texans. It is another one of those recipes that will never quite compare with what a particular Texan grew up on.

Tenderize steak further by pounding to 1/4-inch thickness with a meat mallet. Trim fat. If desired, cut into serving portions.

Blend egg and milk. Salt and pepper meat, dredge in flour, dip in egg-milk mixture, then dredge again in flour.

Skillet fry in 1 inch of hot cooking oil until tender and browned on each side. Drain on paper towels. Serve with Cream Gravy. Serves 4-6.

Cream gravy After cooking chicken-fried steak, pour off all but 2-3 tablespoons of oil while keeping browned flour lying on bottom of skillet. Whisk in 2-3 tablespoons of flour, making a golden roux. Over medium fire, add two cups of milk, stir until mixture boils and is somewhat thick. Add salt; pepper to taste.

- ☒ 2 lbs. top round steak, 1/2-inch thick, tenderized
- ☒ 1 egg
- ☒ 2 tbsps. milk
- ☒ 2 cups all-purpose flour
- ☒ 1/4 cup cooking oil
- ☒ Salt, ground pepper

Cream gravy

- ☒ Leftover grease from chicken-fried steak
- ☒ 2-3 tbsps. flour
- ☒ 2 cups milk
- ☒ Salt; pepper

Fajitas

- ☒ 1-1/2 lbs. skirt steak (substitute flank steak if skirt steak unavailable)
- ☒ Juice of 2-3 limes
- ☒ 1-1/2 tsp. garlic salt
- ☒ 1/2 tsp. pepper

Pico de Gallo
- ☒ 1 cup tomato, chopped
- ☒ 1/4 cup cilantro, chopped
- ☒ 1/2 bell pepper, diced
- ☒ 1/4 cup of tomato juice, or to taste
- ☒ Juice of 1 lemon or lime
- ☒ 3 fresh jalapeños (smoked chipotle peppers if available) seeded, finely chopped
- ☒ 1 medium white onion, coarsely chopped
- ☒ 2 garlic cloves, minced
- ☒ Salt

Few Tex-Mex dishes are as popular as fajitas (fah-HEE-tuzh). Unfortunately, supply and demand then kicked in and the bargain-priced skirt steak, *fajita* in Spanish, became an expensive cut. But worth it. There are chicken and shrimp "fajita" spinoffs, but this recipe is for the original beef.

Trim excess fat and gristle.

Pound to a 1/4-inch thickness, place in plastic sack and sprinkle both sides of steak with lime juice, garlic salt and pepper. Securely tie bag and refrigerate 6-8 hours. Drain off marinade.

Grill whole, preferably over mesquite coals or in a greased skillet. Cut into thin strips.

Serve in warm flour tortillas along with pico de gallo (below), grilled onions, guacamole and sour cream.

Pico de Gallo Mix all ingredients. Chill at least 25 minutes, serve.

Quesadillas

As simple as making a toasted cheese sandwich, this Tex Mex dish makes a perfect snack, canape or lunch entrée.

Generously cover half of the tortillas with grated cheese, or slices of cheese, then fold each.

Melt butter, margarine or oil in a heavy skillet.

Grill each quesadilla until slightly browned, and cheese melted.

⭐ **CORDON BUBBA TIP**

Add chopped onions, jalapeño slices, mushrooms or diced green peppers to cheese before folding.

⭐ 1-1/2 cups of grated Monterey jack or white Mexican cheese

⭐ 2 tbsps. of butter, margarine or oil

⭐ 4 regular-sized flour tortillas

Migas *Tex-Mex omelette*

- 5 corn tortillas, cut into 1/4-inch strips
- 1 onion, chopped
- 1 or 2 jalapeños, finely chopped
- 2 medium tomatoes, diced
- 1/2 bunch of cilantro
- 4 eggs
- 1/4 cup milk
- 1/2 tsp. salt
- 1/4 tsp. pepper
- Juice from 1/2 of a lime

Contributed by Ralph Lauer, Fort Worth

Ralph is some sort of renaissance Texan. Not only a gifted photojournalist and studio photographer, Ralph is an accomplished cook and mountain biker who, in his spare time, keeps a 1950s-era British sports car running.

In a frying pan, combine first five ingredients with a pat of butter on medium heat and sauté for a few minutes till onions soften.

In a small bowl combine eggs, milk, salt and pepper; whisk briskly.

Combine with vegetables in frying pan and fold over until eggs are firm.

Sprinkle with lime juice and serve with a sprig of fresh cilantro.

Oven brisket

Contributed by Jacqueline Smith Glauberman, Dallas

Remove fat from brisket. Salt and pepper meat.

Braise in a roasting pan on high heat until browned.

Line onion slices on top of meat, celery stalks on top of onions. Pour beer over all the ingredients.

Cook in preheated oven at 375 degrees for at least four hours or until meat is tender.

Add 1 cup of water after 1-1/2 hours. Occasionally baste meat with pan juices.

Add potatoes after meat has cooked for 2 hours.

Let meat rest for 20 minutes before slicing. Garnish with chopped parsley. Slice, serve, enjoy.

- 1 4-lb. brisket
- 10 celery stalks
- 2 onions, cut into 1/4-inch slices
- 1 bottle of Heinz chili sauce
- 1 Lone Star beer long-neck
- Salt and pepper to taste
- 6 baking potatoes, quartered

Short-cut bbq brisket

- 5 cups of mesquite (or hickory) chips
- 4 lbs. brisket
- 2 tbsps. coarse pepper
- 2 tbsps. salt
- 1 tsp. cayenne pepper
- Charcoal briquets

Soak chips in water for 1 hour.

Season brisket with salt, pepper and cayenne; let stand 30 minutes.

Pile charcoal briquets at one end of grill and light. When coals are white hot, grill brisket 6 minutes on each side, remove.

Drain water from mesquite chips, and pour chips over coals.

Return grill and place brisket away from coals and chips, cover grill (with vent open) and smoke brisket for 50 minutes.

Preheat oven to 325 degrees, place brisket in baking pan, cover with foil and bake for 4 hours. Slice across the grain; serve immediately.

Use Blackman bbq sauce as a dipping "sop." See next recipe.

Blackman bbq sauce

Contributed by Vickie Blackman Walker, Anson and Fort Worth. A Blackman family favorite, this sauce is great for basting, even better as a sop for dipping.

Combine in a saucepan, simmer 10 minutes.

Brush on chicken, pork or beef halfway through grilling, or use it as a dipping sauce for barbecued brisket.

- ★ 2/3 cup ketchup
- ★ 1/2 cup red wine vinegar
- ★ 8 tsps. Worcestershire sauce
- ★ 1/2 cup brown sugar
- ★ 1 tbsp. dry mustard
- ★ 2 tbsps. chili powder
- ★ 1/2 tsp. ginger
- ★ 1 clove garlic, minced
- ★ 2 tbsps. butter
- ★ 2 slices lemon

Pecan-crusted catfish

- ⭐ 1/3 cup coarse mustard
- ⭐ 1/4 cup Dijon-style mustard
- ⭐ 1/4 cup dry white wine
- ⭐ 1 cup coarsely ground, lightly toasted pecans
- ⭐ 2 large cloves garlic, finely minced
- ⭐ 1/2 cup seasoned bread crumbs
- ⭐ 1 lb. catfish fillets

Preheat oven to 375 degrees.

Thoroughly mix mustards, wine and garlic in small bowl. Set aside.

Mix bread crumbs and pecans together in a large flat plate.

Pat fillets dry with paper towels. Dip each fillet in mustard mixture, then press into the pecan/crumb mixture, creating a heavy crust.

Place on a flat baking pan. Bake 30 to 45 minutes, depending on thickness of fillets.

Pepper steak

Mix steak rub ingredients.

Sprinkle rub generously on meat, covering completely. Let sit for 20 minutes.

Baste meat with butter over open flame, charring outside.

Place steaks over low coals to smoke until done. Cook 10 to 15 minutes on each side for medium rare.

- ☒ Tenderloin steaks, or favorite cut, 1-inch thick
- ☒ Butter

Steak rub
- ☒ 2 tsps. corn starch or flour
- ☒ 2 tsp. salt
- ☒ 2-1/2 tbsps. coarse ground pepper
- ☒ 1/2 tsp. lemon pepper
- ☒ 4 tsps. garlic powder
- ☒ 2 tsps. onion powder
- ☒ 1 tsp. beef stock base (granulated)

Championship chili #1

- 🎱 2 lbs. coarse ground chopped sirloin

- 🎱 Olive oil or butter

- 🎱 1-2 small cans tomato paste, with water (OR fresh tomatoes, finely chopped) (OR canned tomatoes pressed through a colander

- 🎱 3-4 medium onions, chopped

- 🎱 1 bell pepper, chopped

- 🎱 2-10 cloves garlic, minced

- 🎱 1 tbsp. oregano

- 🎱 1/2 tsp. sweet basil

- 🎱 1 tbsp. ground cumin

- 🎱 Salt and pepper to taste

- 🎱 3 tbsps. (or more) chili powder OR some chili pods

Chili tastes different in Texas, where its preparation is a serious undertaking and arguments can ensue over just what needs to be included. One thing that's not is beans. That's a separate dish. Chili is loved and revered the length and breadth of the Lone Star state; there's little doubt why the Legislature voted it the official dish of Texas. That's part of the reason why we've included several recipes, including award-winning ones.

H. Allen Smith's Austin Chili. Tied for 1st Place, 1st World Championship, International Chili Society Cookoff

In a quart pot, brown meat in oil or butter, or in a blend of the two.

Add the remaining ingredients.

Simmer 2-3 hours with the lid on.

Championship chili #2

Dusty Hudspeth's Bottom of the Barrel Gang Chili. Winner, 18th Annual World Championship, International Chili Society Cookoff

Sear meat in covered 2-quart pan with oil.

Add tomato sauce, onion, garlic powder; cover and simmer for 30 minutes, stirring occasionally.

Add remaining ingredients and stir; simmer for one hour.

Add water if necessary.

Serve with side dishes of pinto beans, chopped onions and grated Cheddar cheese for garnishes. Enjoy!

Serves 6-8.

- ⭐ 2 lbs. beef, chili grind
- ⭐ 1 8-oz. can Hunt's tomato sauce
- ⭐ 1 onion, finely chopped
- ⭐ 1 tsp. garlic powder
- ⭐ 1/4 cup Gebhardt Chili Powder
- ⭐ 1 tsp. oregano
- ⭐ 1-1/2 tsps. salt
- ⭐ 2 tsps. ground cumin
- ⭐ 1/4 tsp. cayenne pepper
- ⭐ 1/2 can beer
- ⭐ 1 tbsp. Wesson oil

⭐ **CORDON BUBBA TIP**

Most chili recipes are acidic, so use stainless steel or ceramic coated pots — not cast iron, which might leave a metallic taste. Garnish with raw onions, grated cheese; serve with saltines.

Championship chili #3

- ★ 1 tbsp. oregano
- ★ 2 tbsps. paprika and MSG
- ★ 11 tbsps. Gebhardt Chili Powder
- ★ 4 tbsps. cumin and beef bouillon (instant, crushed)
- ★ 3 cans beer
- ★ 2 lbs. butterfly pork chops, cubed
- ★ 2 lbs. chuck, cubed
- ★ 6 lbs. ground rump
- ★ 4 large onions, finely chopped
- ★ 1/2 cup vegetable oil
- ★ 1 tsp. powdered *mole*
- ★ 10 cloves garlic, minced
- ★ 1 tbsp. sugar
- ★ 2 tsps. coriander seeds
- ★ 1 tsp. Tabasco sauce
- ★ 1 8-oz. can Hunt's tomato sauce
- ★ 1 tbsp. *masa harina* (corn) flour
- ★ Salt to taste

Texan Bill Pfeiffer. Winner, 16th Annual World Championship International Chili Society Cookoff

Mix paprika, oregano, MSG, chili powder, cumin, bouillon, beer and two cups of water. Simmer.

In a separate skillet, brown 1-1/2 lbs. meat with 1 tablespoon oil until meat is light brown. Drain and add to simmering spices. Continue until all meat is added.

Sauté onions and garlic in 1 tablespoon oil. Add spices and meat mixture. Add water as needed. Simmer 2 hours.

Add *mole*, sugar, coriander and tomato sauce.

Dissolve *masa harina* in warm water to form paste, add to chili. Salt to taste.

Simmer 30 minutes. For hotter chili, add more Tabasco.

East meets West Texas chili

Contributed by Vickie Blackman Walker
Anson and Fort Worth

Sauté meat, onion and garlic.

Drain off fat.

Put in a pot, combine remaining
ingredients except beer. Simmer
slowly for at least two hours.

Use beer to thin out to desired
consistency and to drink along
the way.

- ☒ 1-1/2 lbs. ground beef
- ☒ 1-1/2 lbs. coarse ground (chili grind) beef
- ☒ 1 large onion, diced
- ☒ Juice of 1 lemon
- ☒ 2 tbsps. *masa* (Mexican corn flour)
- ☒ 1 15-oz. can tomato sauce
- ☒ 4 tbsps. chili powder
- ☒ 1 tbsp. cumin
- ☒ Salt, pepper to taste
- ☒ 2 cloves of garlic, minced
- ☒ 1/2 tsp. dried oregano and cayenne pepper, or to taste
- ☒ 1/4 tsp. red pepper flakes
- ☒ 1 tbsp. Tabasco sauce
- ☒ 1 square of unsweetened baking chocolate
- ☒ Beer

Cowboy stew

- ☒ 4 lbs. of beef stew meat, 2-inch cubes
- ☒ Flour
- ☒ 4 tbsps. vegetable oil
- ☒ 4 cups water
- ☒ 1 garlic pod
- ☒ 2 bay leaves
- ☒ 1 onion
- ☒ 4 tsps. salt
- ☒ 6 large carrots, sliced
- ☒ 2 cups celery, sliced
- ☒ 8 medium potatoes
- ☒ 2 4-1/2-oz. cans chopped green chilies

Contributed by Sondra Cochran, Fort Worth and Stamford

Dredge meat in flour and brown in oil.

Add water, bay leaves, salt and garlic. Cover and simmer 1-1/2 hours.

Remove bay leaves. Add onions, carrots, potatoes and green chilies.

Add water to cover and cook 30 minutes or until vegetables are done.

Mix 3 tablespoons of flour with 1/2 cup water. Add to stew and simmer until thickened.

Serves 8.

Frito pie

Some people might turn up their noses on a dish more likely found in a school cafeteria than a fine eatery. But too many Texans have been reared on the stuff. And it just happens to be delectable.

Preheat oven to 350 degrees.

Grease a large casserole; cover bottom with corn chips, then a layer of onion, then the chili.

Top with rest of chips. Sprinkle top generously with cheese.

Bake 15 minutes.

- ⭐ 2 tbsps. sweet butter
- ⭐ 5 cups corn chips, broken tostados or taco shells
- ⭐ 2 cups chopped onion
- ⭐ 4 cups chili con carne
- ⭐ 1-1/2 cups each grated Monterey jack and Cheddar, mixed

Jalapeño pie

- 🗹 1 9-in pie shell
- 🗹 1-1/2 cups grated Cheddar, or mixture of Cheddar and Monterrey jack
- 🗹 3/4 cup canned jalapeños, chopped
- 🗹 4 eggs
- 🗹 1/8 cumin powder
- 🗹 1/2 tsp. garlic powder
- 🗹 1/2 tsp. salt

Texas cowboys do eat quiche; they just don't call it that...

Preheat oven at 350 degrees. In pie shell, layer cheese and jalapeños, making sure that cheese tops it.

Beat eggs well, mix in salt and spices.

Pour eggs over all and bake for 30-35 minutes.

King Ranch-style chicken

You can have your coq au vin and your chicken Kiev; make mine King Ranch chicken. A comfort food good enough to feed polite company.

Cut chicken into bite-size pieces, mix with onion and green pepper.

Soak tortillas in boiling broth until soft, then remove.

Mix spices and grated cheese with mushroom soup and sprinkle over alternating layers of chicken and tortillas.

On top, sprinkle tomatoes and chilies.

Bake uncovered at 375 degrees for 30 minutes.

- 3-4 lbs. chicken, boiled and deboned
- 2 medium onions, diced
- 1 can cream of mushroom soup
- 1 can of chicken broth, or liquid from cooking chicken
- Garlic salt, pepper to taste
- 1 green pepper, diced
- 1-1/2 tsps. chili powder, or to taste
- 8 oz. Cheddar cheese, grated
- 12 flour tortillas
- 1 10-oz. can tomatoes with green chilies

Stacked Enchiladas

- ☒ 1 lb. ground beef
- ☒ 1 clove garlic, minced
- ☒ 1 cup onion, chopped
- ☒ 1 green pepper
- ☒ 1/4 cup fresh cilantro
- ☒ 1/4 tsp. ground cumin
- ☒ 1/4 tsp. dried coriander
- ☒ 1 tsp. garlic powder
- ☒ 1/4 cup picante sauce
- ☒ 1 tsp. powdered Worcestershire
- ☒ 1/4 cup chopped black olives
- ☒ 2 tbsps. chili sauce
- ☒ 10-14 corn tortillas
- ☒ 3 cups shredded Cheddar

Sour Cream Sauce

- ☒ 1 stick butter
- ☒ 2 tbsp. flour
- ☒ 1-1/2 cups milk
- ☒ 1 pint sour cream

Contributed by Sharon Clark, Granbury

Brown beef with onion, green pepper and fresh garlic.

While beef is browning, soak corn tortillas in a mixture of water and additional picante sauce.

To browned meat mixture, add remaining ingredients and let cook on low heat for 3 minutes.

Drain water and picante sauce mixture from tortillas.

Layer a 10-by-13-inch casserole with tortillas, meat, cheese. Repeat so there are two layers of meat. End with tortillas.

Top with sour cream sauce and cheese.

Bake at 375 degrees for 25 minutes.

Sour Cream Sauce Melt butter, slowly add remaining ingredients. Stir continuously until smooth.

Grilled quail

Contributed by Grady H. Spears, chef, Reata Restaurant, Alpine and Fort Worth

Rinse quail under cold water, pat dry. Arrange in large, shallow baking pan.

Add 1/4 cup oil, 1/4 cup thyme leaves and 1/4 teaspoon pepper to pan. Coat quail thoroughly.

Cover and refrigerate up to 24 hours. Return meat to room temperature.

Heat grill to medium hot.

Sprinkle quail with salt.

Grill quail breast side first until golden brown and cooked through, 12 to 15 minutes per side.

- ☒ 12 quail, about 1/2 lb. each
- ☒ 1/4 cup olive oil
- ☒ 1/4 cup loosely packed thyme leaves
- ☒ 1/4 tsp. freshly ground black pepper
- ☒ Salt

Son-of-a-gun stew

- 1/4 lb. beef suet, finely chopped
- 1 calf heart, cut in small pieces
- 1 calf liver, cut in small pieces
- 2 calf kidneys, cut in small pieces
- Marrow gut, chopped
- 1 lb. veal sweetbreads, simmered in salt water, membrane removed
- 1/2 lb. beef brain, soaked in salt water, deveined and cubed
- 2 onions, chopped
- 1 can of tomatoes
- 2 cups beef broth
- 1/2 cup flour, blended with hot water
- Salt, to taste

A.k.a. Sonofoabitch Stew. It didn't get much better than this on a cattle drive. This is genuine chuckwagon fare.

In a large Dutch oven, melt beef suet.

Add and sear heart, liver, kidneys and marrow gut.

Add remaining ingredients.

Cover, cook 2 hours or until meat is tender.

Tamales

A task to make, but it's a dish many Texans yearn for during the year-end holidays. Good anytime.

Trim edges of corn husks if needed, soak in hot water for several hours to soften. Pat dry.

Cook pork (or beef) till tender, drain and retain broth, cool. Shred meat. Melt lard or (pour oil) in heavy skillet. Add spices, then meat and stir over low heat until well blended.

Dough: Mix remaining ingredients, using just enough water to make a non-sticking, soft dough.

TAMALE ASSEMBLY

On each softened corn husk, spread a tablespoon or more of dough on the smooth side. Add about a tablespoon of meat filling on top of dough. Roll husk so that meat mixture is enclosed, fold up bottom end. Stand tamales, open end up, in a steamer basket or pot rack; cover with damp cloth. Add water to a level of 2 inches. Cover and steam 50 minutes or until done.

- 1 package of dried corn husks,
- 2 lbs. boneless pork (shoulder or center rib) or beef shoulder
- 3 tbsps. lard or vegetable oil
- 1 tsp. cumin
- 2 tsps. cayenne
- 1 garlic clove, minced
- 1 cup diced onion
- Salt, pepper to taste
- 4 cups *masa harina* flour
- 3 cups hot low-salt chicken or pork broth
- 1/2 cup shortening
- 1 tsp. salt
- 1 tsp. baking powder
- 1 tbsp. chili powder

Texas hash

- 1-1/2 lbs. ground beef
- 2 tbsps. vegetable oil
- 1 clove garlic, minced
- 2 onions, chopped
- 2 green bell peppers, chopped
- 1 16-oz. can tomatoes
- 1 tsp. chili powder
- Salt and black pepper, to taste
- 2/3 cup uncooked rice
- Grated cheese, as garnish

Brown garlic, then beef in pot or large skillet with oil.

Add onion and green bell pepper, and cook till tender.

Drain fat. Add spices and tomatoes and bring to boil.

Stir in rice, cover and simmer for 30 minutes, stirring occasionally.

Garnish with grated cheese.

Serves 5-6

Beans and rice

Soak washed beans in water overnight.

Put drained beans, onions, garlic and spices into pot, cover with water.

After bringing to a boil, simmer until beans are tender.

Cook rice separately.

Add sliced sausage to tender bean mixture and cook 25 minutes.

Serve in chili bowls over rice.

- 3 cups of cooked rice
- 2 cups of dried red beans, or pinto beans, depending on what your grandmother used
- 2 cloves garlic
- 2 tbsps. vegetable oil
- 1 bay leaf
- 2 large onions
- 1-1/2 tsps. cumin
- 1 smoked sausage
- Cayenne pepper, or chili powder, to taste
- Salt, black pepper to taste

Fried catfish

- ☒ 2 lbs. catfish, cut into 1/2-by-4-inch strips
- ☒ 1/4 cup red wine vinegar
- ☒ 1 tsp. each salt and pepper
- ☒ 1 tsp. each: garlic powder, onion powder, cayenne pepper
- ☒ 1 cup Creole mustard
- ☒ 2 eggs
- ☒ 5 to 6 dashes Tabasco
- ☒ 1 cup yellow corn flour
- ☒ 1/3 cup yellow cornmeal

Texas Tartar Sauce
- ☒ 1 cup mayonnaise
- ☒ 1 tbsp. fresh lemon juice
- ☒ 2 tbsps. dill pickle relish
- ☒ 1 tbsp. each chopped jalapeño, chopped capers, chopped celery
- ☒ 1/2 tbsp. each salt, pepper, Creole mustard
- ☒ 2 or 3 dashes green jalapeño Tabasco

Contributed by Lubbock native Keith Faulkner, chef of New Orleans' Plimsoll Club

Combine vinegar; 1 teaspoon each of salt, pepper, garlic and onion powder; 1 cup Creole mustard; eggs and Tabasco.

Marinate catfish in mixture for 30 minutes.

In separate bowl, make breading by combining corn flour, cornmeal, 1 teaspoon of salt, pepper and cayenne pepper. Roll fish in breading.

Fry in vegetable oil at 375 degrees for 3 to 5 minutes or until done.

Serve with Texas Tartar sauce.

Texas Tartar Sauce Combine all ingredients.

Posole

Boil six cups of water, add pork, one bay leaf, one serrano pepper, one minced garlic clove, and one diced tomato.

Simmer 30 minutes over low heat. Drain water.

Add six cups of fresh water, hominy, three chopped tomatoes, carrots, two peppers, one minced garlic clove, bay leaf, cayenne, black pepper and lime juice.

Cover and simmer over low heat 60 minutes.

Serve with diced radishes, shredded lettuce, sliced green onions as garnish and wedges of lime.

- 3 lbs. lean pork loin, cubed into small pieces
- 12 cups water
- 3 15-oz. cans hominy
- 1/4 cup chopped cilantro (fresh coriander)
- 4 medium diced tomatoes
- 2 diced carrots
- 3 diced serrano peppers
- 2 garlic cloves, minced
- 6 bay leaves
- 1 tsp. cayenne
- Salt, pepper, to taste
- Juice of 1 lime

Puddin'
AND PIES

★ DESSERTS

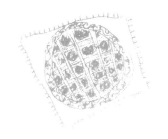

Bourbon chocolate pecan pie

Preheat oven to 375 degrees.

Cream sugar and butter, combine with corn syrup, eggs, salt, vanilla and bourbon.

Mix pecan pieces and chocolate morsels, then spread on bottom of pie shell.

Pour over filling.

Bake for 40-45 minutes, or until set.

- ☒ 1/4 cup butter
- ☒ 1 cup sugar
- ☒ 3 eggs, lightly beaten
- ☒ 3/4 cup light corn syrup
- ☒ 1/4 tsp. salt
- ☒ 3 tbsps. bourbon, or to taste
- 1 tsp. vanilla extract
- ☒ 3/4 cup chopped pecans
- ☒ 3/4 cup semi-sweet chocolate morsels
- ☒ 1 9-inch pie shell

Bread pudding

- ☒ 1 pan of stale (French) bread, cut into 1-inch cubes
- ☒ 1/2 gallon milk
- ☒ 1-1/2 lbs. sugar
- ☒ 9 eggs
- ☒ 1 tbsp. each vanilla, cinnamon
- ☒ 1 tsp. powdered ginger
- ☒ 1/2 tsp. nutmeg
- ☒ 2 bananas, sliced
- ☒ 1 pint strawberries, quartered
- ☒ 1/2 cup each blueberries, raisins, coconut shavings

Whiskey Sauce

- ☒ 1 cup sugar
- ☒ 1/2 cup butter
- ☒ 1/4 cup water
- ☒ 2 oz. whiskey, or to taste

Contributed by Keith Faulkner, Lubbock and New Orleans

Soak bread in milk for 30 minutes.

In a bowl, mix sugar, eggs, vanilla, cinnamon, ginger and nutmeg. Whip to combine.

Add the fruit to the soggy bread and fold in the egg mixture.

Bake in a 9-by-18-by-2-inch pan at 350 degrees for 1-1/2 hours.

Top with whiskey sauce.

Serves 12 to 20.

Whiskey Sauce In sauce pan or double boiler, whisk sugar into melted butter until sugar is dissolved. Add water and blend. Remove from heat and add whiskey.

Flan *(Creme caramel au Tex Mex)*

Sprinkle sugar in a heavy skillet; stir over low heat until melted.

Remove from heat when caramelized golden brown, then pour into 9-inch cake pan.

Allow to cool. Blend milk, sweetened condensed milk, salt, vanilla, almond extract and eggs extremely well, then pour over caramelized sugar.

Place cake pan in larger pan filled to 1 inch with hot water.

Cover pan with foil. Bake at 350 degrees for 1 hour or until knife comes out clean.

Cut into serving squares.

⭐ 1/2 cup sugar

⭐ 3 whole eggs and 3 additional yolks

⭐ Pinch of salt

⭐ 1 14-oz.can sweetened condensed milk

⭐ 1 cup milk

⭐ 1 tsp. vanilla

⭐ 1/2 tsp. almond extract

⭐ **CORDON BUBBA TIP**

At first step, add an ounce of rum, brandy, Amaretto, Kahlua, or your favorite liqueur.

Peach cobbler

Pastry

- ☒ 3/4 cup shortening
- ☒ 3 cups flour
- ☒ 1-1/2 tsp. salt
- ☒ 8 tbsps. cold water
- ☒ 2 tsps. baking powder

Filling

- ☒ 8 cups of fresh sliced peaches
- ☒ 2 tbsps. lemon juice
- ☒ 4 tbsps. butter
- ☒ 2 cups sugar
- ☒ 4 tbps. flour
- ☒ 1/2 tbsp. vanilla
- ☒ 1 tsp. almond extract
- ☒ 1/2 tbsp. nutmeg
- ☒ 1 tsp. cinnamon
- ☒ 1 tbsp. cornstarch

PASTRY: Mix flour, salt, baking powder until blended coarsely. Sprinkle with water, then mash mixture until moist.

FILLING: Mix flour, sugar, then gradually add water, nutmeg, vanilla, almond extract, cinnamon, cornstarch, lemon juice. Add peaches. Let stand.

Take three-fourths of pastry and roll out to pie crust thickness, then use it to line a 13-by-9 inch or equivalent greased baking dish. Ladle in peach mixture. Roll out remainder of pastry to pie crust thickness, cut into strips and arrange latticework design over top of peaches. Bake at 350 degrees for 1 hour, or until top of cobbler is browned.

Pecan pie

Contributed by Sondra Cochran, , Fort Worth
and Stamford

Allow butter to cool, then combine all
ingredients, mixing well.

Pour into a 9-inch uncooked pie shell.

Bake at 350 degrees for 50 minutes or
until toothpick comes out clean.

- 1 stick of butter or margarine, melted
- 1 cup light brown sugar
- 1 cup light corn syrup
- 1/8 tsp. salt
- 4 eggs, well beaten
- 1-1/2 cups chopped pecans
- 1 tsp. vanilla
- 1 9-inch uncooked pie shell

Chess pie

- ⭐ 9-inch pie shell, unbaked
- ⭐ 1 tbsp., plus 1 tsp. of cornmeal
- ⭐ 1/2 cup butter
- ⭐ 1 tbsp. apple cider vinegar
- ⭐ 3 eggs
- ⭐ 1-1/2 cups sugar
- ⭐ 1/2 tsp. vanilla

A Stringer family recipe, Young County

Chill pie shell.

Preheat oven to 350 degrees.

Combine, then beat ingredients. Pour into pie shell and bake for 50 to 55 minutes, or until firm.

Ambrosia

Contributed by Georgia White of Bonham

Use enough hot water to dissolve gelatin fully , then blend with cream cheese until smooth.

Add 2 cups cold water.

Let mixture partly jell in the refrigerator. Then add the remaining ingredients.

Let sit in the refrigerator about 2 hours before serving.

- ⚝ 1 large box of orange gelatin
- ⚝ 4 oz. cream cheese
- ⚝ 25 small marshmallows
- ⚝ 1 (15-oz.) can of crushed pineapple
- ⚝ 1 cup of chopped pecans
- ⚝ 1 tub of whipped cream topping substitute

Sour milk cookies

- ⊠ 1 cup shortening
- ⊠ 2 cups sugar
- ⊠ 3 eggs
- ⊠ 1-1/2 tsps. vanilla
- ⊠ 4 cups flour
- ⊠ 1 tsp. baking powder
- ⊠ 1/4 tsp. baking soda
- ⊠ 1/4 cup sour milk or buttermilk

Circa 1910 recipe by Nannie Akers, Fort Worth and Eliasville, handed down to her granddaughters.

Cream shortening and sugar; beat until light and fluffy.

Add well-beaten eggs, milk and vanilla.

Sift together flour, baking powder, baking soda and salt, then add to creamed mixture.

Roll out and cut into cookie shapes, or drop by spoonfuls on baking sheet and mark a cross with fork.

Bake 8 minutes at 350 degrees.

Pecan cake

By Emma Jean Stringer Fitzgerald, Stringer Family Recipes

Beat sugar, eggs and butter until fluffy, then alternately mix in portions of the baking powder, 3-1/2 cups of flour and lemon extract.

Then mix 1/2 cup of flour, pecans, raisins and add to the first mixture.

Bake in a tube pan at 325 degrees for 1 hour 45 minutes.

- 2 cups sugar
- 6 eggs
- 2 cups butter
- 1-1/2 tsps. baking powder
- 4 cups flour
- 2 oz. of lemon extract
- 4 cups chopped pecans
- 2-1/2 cups raisins

Pecan tart

Crust

- ☒ 1-1/2 cups all-purpose flour
- ☒ 1/2 cup butter (or margarine)
- ☒ 1/4 tsp. salt
- ☒ 1 egg
- ☒ 1/4 cup granulated sugar

Filling

- ☒ 2 cups of Texas pecan halves or pieces
- ☒ 1 cup brown sugar
- ☒ 2 eggs
- ☒ 1/2 tsp. baking powder
- ☒ 1/2 cup all-purpose flour
- ☒ 1/2 tsp. cinnamon

Crust: Preheat oven to 400 degrees.

Hand-whisk all ingredients or mix at slow speed.

With dough, line bottom and 1 inch up sides of a 10-inch fluted tart pan, preferably with detachable bottom, or greased pan of similar size.

Bake for 8 to 10 minutes and remove.

Filling: Mix eggs and brown sugar until fluffy.

Add flour, cinnamon, baking powder and pecans, then spread into prepared crust.

Bake at 350 degrees for about 30 minutes or until center is firm.

Sweet potato pie

Preheat oven to 450 degrees.

Mash potatoes, mixing in spices, corn starch and sugar; blend well.

Mix in milk. Beat eggs, then add to mixture.

Melt butter and add. Pour mixture into pie shell and place in oven.

Bake at 450 degrees for 10 minutes; reduce heat to 350 degrees and bake another 30 minutes, or until center is set and crust is brown.

- 2 cups cooked, peeled, mashed sweet potatoes
- 1 tsp. grated nutmeg
- 1 tsp. cinnamon
- 1 tsp. vanilla
- 2 tsps. corn starch
- 1 cup brown sugar
- 1 cup milk
- 3 eggs
- 4 tbsps. butter
- 9-in unbaked pie shell

Kolaches

Sweet dough

- ☒ 2 packages dry yeast
- ☒ 1/4 cup warm water
- ☒ 1/2 cup sugar
- ☒ 2 cups milk
- ☒ 1/2 cup butter
- ☒ 2 tbsps. sugar
- ☒ 2 tsps. salt
- ☒ 6-1/4 cups sifted flour
- ☒ 2 egg yolks, slightly beaten

Filling

- ☒ 1-1/2 cups milk
- ☒ 1-1/4 cups sugar
- ☒ 1 tbsp. flour
- ☒ 1 cup ground poppy seeds
- ☒ 1 tbsp. butter
- ☒ 1 tsp. vanilla

A Czech-Tex pastry by Claudia Matacek, Grand Champion, 1987 Kolache Capital Cookoff, Caldwell

Dissolve yeast in warm water. Add 1 tablespoon sugar and let stand.

Heat milk until almost scalding. Remove from heat and stir in butter, 1/2 cup sugar. Cool to lukewarn and add yeast mixture.

In large bowl, combine salt and 5-1/4 cups of flour. Add yeast and milk mixture to flour, mix. Add egg yolks. Mix in enough of last cup of flour till it's workable.

Knead on floured board until glossy. Grease bowl.

Turn dough in bowl to grease. Cover and let rise in warm place until double in bulk. Roll out to about 1/2-inch thick and cut into into individual kolaches with biscuit cutter.

Place on greased pan so not quite touching. Brush with softened butter and let rise again covered until light to the touch. Make indentation in each. Add filling of your choice. Bake in 375-degree oven until brown, about 25 minutes. Remove and brush with softened butter.

Poppy Seed Filling Heat milk and when it boils, add sugar, flour and poppy seeds, stirring vigorously. Cook over medium heat until mixture thickens. Remove from heat. Add butter and then vanilla. Cool filling. Spoon 1 teaspoon of filling onto center top of each kolache.

Peach cobbler ice cream

Contributed by Joe Libowsky, Milwaukee Joe's Gourmet Ice Cream, Bedford and Fort Worth. Joe, a recovering Yankee from Wisconsin, was a federal law-man in Texas until hanging up his holster to pursue a lifelong dream of crafting the world's richest ice cream. He makes a new flavor every day. And peach cobbler, one of the most requested, best reflects his adopted state.

Preheat oven to 350 degrees. In a mixing bowl, add cream cheese and sugar. Mix with hands until sugar is blended. Gradually add flour and mix with hands until blended and mixture will form a ball. If mixture is dry, add water; if too wet, add flour. Knead dough for approximately 30 seconds. With a rolling pin, or by hand, roll out dough until about the thickness of pie crust. Bake on cookie sheet until golden brown, then allow to cool. Cut crust into 1/2-inch pieces.

Puree 1 cup of peaches. Chop remaining 1 cup of peaches into medium-sized pieces and set aside. Pour cream into mixing bowl. Whisk in sugar at little at a time until completely blended. Pour in half-and-half and whisk until blended. Stir in peach puree. Transfer mixture to ice cream maker and freezer, following manufacturer's instructions. After ice cream stiffens, but before becoming completely solid, add chopped peaches and chopped pie crust, then continue to freeze until ice cream is ready. Makes 1 generous quart.

Cobbler crust

- ☒ 4-oz. cream cheese
- ☒ 1/2 cup of sugar
- ☒ 1/2 cup of flour

Peach Ice Cream

- ☒ 2 cups of peaches
- ☒ 2 cups heavy or whipping cream
- ☒ 3/4 cup sugar
- ☒ 2/3 cup of half-and-half

Chasers

BEVERAGES

Aunt Merle's
Easy Margaritas

Mix all ingredients.

For salt on rim, rub a lime rind around the top rim of each glass.

Roll rims into salt (or, as a variation, sugar). Serve over ice.

Makes about a dozen.

- ☒ 12 oz. fresh squeezed lime juice
- ☒ 18 oz. Triple Sec
- ☒ 24 oz. tequila
- ☒ 1 to 1-1/2 cups water

Coosie Arbuckle
Trail coffee

- ☒ Ground coffee
- ☒ Water

"Coosie" was what cowhands called the cook on cattle drives. Arbuckle was the brand of coffee that became the generic name for the morning cup of java on the trail. Both are now gone, but this formula lives on.

Using grandma's dented old blue enamel coffee pot, throw in a heaping tablespoon of coffee for each cup, and an extra tablespoon "for the pot."

Add one cup of water for each serving, and "one for the pot."

Heat slowly over low heat, then bring to a boil. Toss in 1/4 cup cold water to settle grounds.

☒ **CORDON BUBBA TIP**

To enliven coffee, stir in 1/4 teaspoon of ground cinnamon per serving, and you have a chuckwagon version of *cafe caneja*.

Jalapeño martini

Drop jalapeño slices in a bottle of vodka, replace cap and refrigerate 48 hours. (If keeping for more than several days, remove jalapeños.)

For individual martini, swirl vermouth into stemmed cocktail glass, then drain off. Pour 2.5 ounces of chilled jalapeño vodka (over ice, if "on the rocks"), stir and add a sliver of jalapeño as garnish.

☆ 1 750-ml bottle of vodka

☆ 4 jalapeños, seeded and sliced

☆ Dash of vermouth

☆ 1 sliver of jalapeño

Weights & Measures

Cooking Measurment Equivalents

16 tablesppns = 1 cup
12 tablespoons = 3/4 cup
10 tablespoons + 2 teaspoons = 2/3 cup
8 tablespoons = 1/2 cup
6 tablespoons = 3/8 cup
5 tablespoons + 1 teaspoon = 1/3 cup
4 tablespoons = 1/4 cup
2 tablespoons = 1/8 cup
2 tablespoons + 2 teaspoons = 1/6 cup
1 tablespoon = 1/16 cup
2 cups = 1 pint
2 pints = 1 quart
3 teaspoons = 1 tablespoon
48 teaspoons = 1 cup

Metric Equivalents

Capacity
1/5 teaspoon = 1 milliliter
1 teaspoon = 5 ml
1 tablespoon = 15 ml
1/5 cup = 50 ml
1 cup = 240 ml (about 1/4 liter)
2 cups (1 pint) = 470 ml
4 cups (1 quart) = .95 liter
4 quarts (1 gal.) = 3.8 liters

Weight
1 ounce = 30 grams
1 pound = 454 grams

More Weights & Measures

Metric to U.S. Measures

Capacity
   1 militers = 1/5 teaspoon
   5 ml = 1 teaspoon
   15 ml = 1 tablespoon
   34 ml = 1 fluid oz.
   100 ml = 3.4 fluid oz.
   240 ml = 1 cup
   1 liter = 34 fluid oz.
   1 liter = 4.2 cups
   1 liter = 2.1 pints
   1 liter = 1.06 quarts
   1 liter = .26 gallon

Weight
   1 gram = .035 ounce
   100 grams = 3.5 ounces
   500 grams = 1.10 pounds
   1 kilogram = 2.205 pounds
   1 kilogram = 35 oz.

Oven Temperature Guide

	C	F
Warm	150	300
Moderately Warm	160	325
Medium	180	350
Moderately Hot	190	375
Hot	200-210	400-415
Broil	288	550

Cordon Bubba
texas cuisine

Index by Section

Alphabetized Index

Consider other offerings in our Texas & Southwestern line of acclaimed cookbooks

"Small size, big taste!" – Galveston Daily News

Salsa! Salsa! Salsa!
Native Texan Crystal Walls offers 75 different salsas, from traditional favorites to gourmet originals and even dessert varieties. "Hottest book on the shelf!" – Bud Kennedy, Fort Worth Star-Telegram
ISBN 1-892588-05-6. Suggested retail $5.95.

Texas Braggin' Rights
Winning recipes of the best Texas cook-offs, including the State Fair of Texas, Stonewall Peach JAMboree Festival and the Black-Eyed Pea Festival. "Texana for foodies!" – D magazine.
ISBN 1-892588-01-3. Suggested retail $5.95.

Tex Mex 101
This handy guide makes genuine Texan-Mexican cuisine accessible to any kitchen. "From family favorites to gourmet creations – recipes from Texans who know" – Sherman-Denison Herald News
ISBN 1-892588-02-1. Suggested retail $5.95.

Championship Chili
A guide to making chili, using recipes that swept top honors at the leading two national cook-offs. Includes a veteran competitor-judge's secrets on what makes a winning "bowl of blessedness."
ISBN 1-892588-03-X. Suggested retail $5.95.

Texas Morning Glory
Memorable breakfast recipes from Lone Star bed and breakfast inns. All easy to follow, all guaranteed to bring you back for more.
ISBN 1-892588-04-8. Suggested retail $5.95.